Love to Sing an

 Love to Sing

1. Hello Song

New Zealand:
Hello, Hello everybody (2x), Hello

Maori:
Kia Ora, Kia Ora tamariki (2x), Kia Ora

Chinese:
Nee How, Nee how peng yow (2x), Nee how

American:
Hi There, Hi there buddy (2x), Hi there

African:
Jumbo, Jumbo Sanna (2x), Jumbo

Dutch:
Hallo, Hallo beste vriendjes (2x), Hallo

Australian:
G'day, G'day old mate (2x), G'day

Fijian:
Bula, Bula Vinaka (2x), Bula

French:
Bonjour, Bonjour mes amis (2x), Bonjour

Japanese:
Konnichiwa, Dõzo yoroshi ku (2x), Konnichiwa

Samoan:
Talofa, Talofa tamaiti (2x), Talofa

English:
Good Show, Good Show old chappy (2x), Good Show!

Children stand in a line.

Child who sings 'greeting' walks along the line shaking hands with other children

Note: Chinese is phonetically translated from:
你好，朋友，你好
Japanese is phonetically translated from:
こんにちは どうぞ よろしく

2. Pohutukawa Tree

I am a Pohutukawa seed _(B)_
Plant me in the ground and water me _(F#)_
Plenty of sunshine is what I need _(B)_
Then guess what you will see? _(F#7) (B)_

Out will shoot a tiny twig
And it will continue to grow so big
Beautiful flowers of whero
The native tree of Aotearoa.

Pohutukawa tree, Pohutukawa tree _(E) (B)_
New Zealand's Christmas tree _(F#7) (B)_
You fill my heart with aroha _(E) (B)_
The native tree of Aotearoa. _(F#7) (B)_

Point to yourself, spread arms out.

Plant seed in the ground then pretend to pour water from a watering can. Spread out arms and 'twinkle' fingers. Hold out hands

Point up forefinger from the ground.
Stand up tall and spread out arms.
Use hands to form flowers.
Sway side to side with arms held out high.

Sway side to side with arms held out high.

Clasp heart.
Sway side to side with arms held out high.

6

Pohutukawa tree

3. The Jolly Ship

Oh around and around went the jolly, jolly ship
$$\text{D} \qquad\qquad \text{A7} \qquad\qquad \text{D} \qquad \text{A7}$$
Oh around and around went she
$$\text{D} \qquad \text{A7} \qquad\qquad \text{D}$$
Oh around and around went the jolly, jolly ship
$$\text{A7} \qquad\qquad \text{D} \qquad \text{A7}$$
Till she sank to the bottom of the sea.
$$\text{D} \qquad \text{A7} \qquad\qquad \text{D}$$

'Pull her up, pull her up' said the captain of the ship
'Pull her up, pull her up' said she
'Pull her up, pull her up' said the captain of the ship
'Till she pops to the top of the sea!'

Hold hands to form a circle and dance around.

Slowly bend down to a crouch.

Let go of hands.

Pretend to pull a thick rope and show pulling up action.

Jump up!

around and around went the jolly jolly ship

4. Rere Atu (Maori Poi Song)

Lyrics	Translation
Rere atu _(D)	*Twirl poi away from you.*
Rere mai _(G)	*Twirl poi back to you*
Taku poi _(A7)	*Catch poi in other hand, twirl.*
Rere mai _(D)	*Catch poi in other hand, twirl.*
Rere runga _(D)	*Twirl poi up.*
Rere raro _(G)	*Twirl poi down.*
Rere tika e _{(A7) (D)}	*Twirl, catch poi in other hand.*
Rere tika e _{(A7) (D)}	*Twirl, catch poi in other hand.*

Repeat

Fly away
Fly back
My poi
Fly to me
Fly up
Fly down
Fly straight along
Fly true, fly true.

Repeat

Note: second verse is English translation.

10

fly away · fly back · my poi · fly up · fly down

·fly straight along · fly true.

5. In and Out the Dusky Bluebells

In and out the dusky bluebells [D]
In and out the dusky bluebells [A7]
In and out the dusky bluebells [D]
Who shall be my leader? [A7] [D]

Tippety tappety on your shoulder
Tippety tappety on your shoulder
Tippety tappety on your shoulder
You shall be my leader!

Repeat 2x

Children make a circle with hands joined to form arches. One child skips in and out of the arches. At the end of this verse, the child who has been skipping stops behind another.

Tap the new leader on the shoulder.

Hold onto shoulders of new leader and skip in and out of the arches.

·in·and·out·the·dusky·bluebells·

13

6. Punchinello

Look who is here, Punchinello, funny fellow
Look who is here, Punchinello, funny clown.

What can you do, Punchinello, funny fellow?
What can you do, Punchinello, funny clown?

We'll do it too, Punchinello, funny fellow
We'll do it too, Punchinello, funny clown.

Who do you choose, Punchinello, funny fellow?
Who do you choose, Punchinello, funny clown?

Repeat

Children hold hands and dance around in a circle. Chosen child stands in the centre.

Children drop hands, stand still and open arms.

'Punchinello' chooses action (e.g. hopping, turning around etc.) Children do the action as well.

'Punchinello' closes eyes, points out finger, turns around and chooses a new 'Punchinello' at the end of this verse. Children clap hands.

14

Punchinello

funny fellow

15

7. One Little Elephant Balancing

One little elephant balancing, (D) (A7)
Step by step on a piece of string (D)
Thought it was such tremendous fun (A7)
That .... called for another elephant to come! (D)

Two little elephants balancing,
Step by step on a piece of string
Thought it was such tremendous fun
That .... called for another elephant to come!

Three little elephants balancing,
Step by step on a piece of string
Thought it was such tremendous fun
That .... called for another elephant to come!

Use string or draw with chalk to make a circle.
A chosen child walks on the circle and chooses
another child at the end of the verse.

16

One little elephant balancing

17

8. Jimmy Jello

Jimmy Jello ^D wibble ^G wobble
Is ^{A7} an incredibly fl^Dexible fellow
He can do the splits
With his ^G hands on his hips
And b^{A7}alance a banana on his nose
While wriggling his long to^Des.

Marsha Mellow tingle tangle
Is a delightful tap tap dancer
She can tap on the ceiling
While she's cartwheeling
And whistle a melodious tune
About 'Sally Go Round the Moon'.

Clap name and shake body.

Shake arms and legs.

Spread legs apart.

Hands on hips.

Place finger on nose.

Wriggle toes.

Clap name, point out alternate feet.

Tap feet.

Point to ceiling.

Do a cartwheel.

Make a circle with arms.

19

9. The Muffin Man

Oh, have you seen the muffin man [D]
The muffin man, the muffin man [G] [A7]
Oh, have you seen the muffin man [D]
Who lives in Drury Lane O? [G] [A7] [D]

Oh yes, I've seen the muffin man
The muffin man, the muffin man
Oh yes, I've seen the muffin man
Who lives in Drury Lane O.

Children join hands to form a circle. Chosen child is blindfolded and stands in the centre. Everyone sings the question verse. At the end of this verse, the blindfolded child touches someone in the ring. This person sings the response verse, at the end of which the blindfolded child guesses who it can be. If correct, the two children change places.

O have you seen the muffin man

21

10. Ballin' the Jack

First you put your two knees close up tight [C7]
You swing them to the left [F7]
And then you swing them to the right
You step around the floor kind of nice and light [Bb7]
And then you twist around and twist around [Eb] [G7]
With all of your might [Ab7] [G7]
Stretch your loving arms way out in space [C7]
You do the eagle rock with such style and grace [F7]
You swing your foot way out and you swing it back [Ab] [F7] [Eb] [C7]
That's what I call Ballin' the Jack! [F7] [Ab] [Bb7] [Eb]

Repeat 2x

That's what I call Ballin' the Jack!

Put your knees together.

Swing your knees to the left.

Swing your knees to the right.

Step around in your own circle.

Twist up and down.

Stretch arms up high.

Move out-stretched arms up and down.

Swing one foot out and bring it back.

Dance and clap.

23

11. Summer Jive

A ^D jump a jump a jump | Jump up and down.
A turning around and then ^{A7} | Jump around in a circle.
A jump a jump a jump | Jump up and down.
Then do the summer jive! ^D | Click fingers.

Chorus: Rollerblade!   Slide alternate feet and swing alternate arms.
         Starjump!   Do a star jump.
         Dive bomb!   Block nose and crouch to a squat.
         Stargaze!   Lie flat on your back.
         Fly a kite!   Fly a pretend kite.

A hop a hop a hop | Hop on one foot.
A turning around and then | Hop on one foot in a circle.
A hop a hop a hop | Hop on one foot.
Then do the summer jive! | Click fingers.

Repeat chorus

A shake a shake a shake | Shake your whole body.
A turning around and then | Shake your body and turn in a circle.
A shake a shake a shake | Shake your whole body.
Then do the summer jive! | Click fingers.

Repeat chorus.

24

12. Boomps - a - Daisy

Hands, knees and boomps - a - daisy! [C] [G7] [C] [A7]
I like a bustle that bends [Dm] [A7] [Dm]
Hands, knees and boomps - a - daisy! [G7] [Am] [Cm]
What is a boomp between friends? [G] [D7] [G7]
La, la, la, la, la
Hands, knees oh don't be lazy [C] [G7] [C] [A7]
Let's make the party a wow! [Dm] [A7] [Dm]
Now then hands, knees and boomps - a - daisy! [F] [F#d:m] [C] [A7]
Turn to your partner and bow. [Dm] [G7] [C]

Repeat

Bow-wow! [G7] [C]

A partner is required.

Slap partner's hands, slap own knees, then bump bottoms with partner. Bend down.

Slap partner's hands, slap own knees, then bump bottoms with partner. Bump bottoms together. Twirl hands.

Slap partner's hands, slap own knees, shake head and shake index finger. Raise arms, sway side to side.

Slap partner's hands, slap own knees, then bump bottoms with partner. Bow to your partner.

Bow to your partner.

hands, knees and boomps-a daisy

13. Hokey Tokey

You put your right arm in [Bb]
You put your right arm out
You put your right arm in
And you shake is all about [F7]
You do the Hokey Tokey
And you turn yourself around
That's what it's all about. [Bb]

Chorus: Oh Hokey Hokey Tokey [Bb]
                Oh Hokey Hokey Tokey [F7]
                Oh Hokey Hokey Tokey [Bb] [Eb7]
                And that's what it's all about! [F7] [Bb]

You put your left arm in...
Repeat Chorus.
You put your right leg in...
Repeat Chorus.
You put your left leg in...
Repeat Chorus.
You put your whole self in...
Repeat Chorus.

And that's what it's all about!
And that's what it's all about! Yeah!

Stand in a circle and do the actions as suggested by the words.

Hold hands up and sway body side to side.
Turn around in a circle.
Clap hands.

Holding hands, dance into the middle then back out again.

Clap hands.

Actions as suggested by words.

Clap hands.
Clap hands. Jump up into the air.

Shake it all about

14. Limbo Rock

Every limbo boy and girl
^B
All around the limbo world
Gonna do the limbo rock
All around the limbo clock
Jack be limbo Jack be quick
Jack go under limbo stick
All around the limbo clock
Hey let's do the limbo rock!

Limbo lower now
Limbo lower now
How low can you go?

First you spread your limbo feet
Then you move to limbo beat
Limbo ankle limbo knee
Bend back like the limbo tree
Jack be limbo Jack be quick
Jack go under limbo stick
All around the limbo clock
Hey let's do the limbo rock!

Don't move that limbo bar
You'll be a limbo star
How low can you go?

Two people hold the ends of a 'broom stick'. Children go under one at a time. You can do the traditional limbo or do variations. Instead of bending back think of different ways of going under the limbo stick. (e.g. slide or roll under.)

15. Statue Song

C#m9
Get down and boogie, get down and boogie
Shake it up! ☆☆☆
Go with the flow! ☆☆☆
Hang loose just like a long neck goose
We're playing statues, we're playing statues
We're playing the statue song - oh yeah!

Everybody join on in, everybody join on in
☆☆☆ Freeze!
☆☆☆ Breathe and blink
Hang loose just like a long neck goose
Don't move a muscle, don't move a muscle
We're playing the statue song - oh yeah!

Don't be a party pooper, don't be a party pooper
Hey cool cat! ☆☆☆
You're real choice! ☆☆☆
Hang loose just like a long neck goose
We're having a good time, we're having a great time
We're playing the statue song - oh yeah!

You're out!
I have to say
I love the smile on your face
Isn't it great!
You're such a good sport!

Repeat first verse.

NB: ☆ means a single clap.

Children dance to the music. A person stops the music so that the children have to 'freeze'. If a child moves he/she is out and can help to be a judge.

33

16. Alice the Camel

Alice the camel has five humps [D]
Alice the camel has five humps [A7] [D]
Alice the camel has five humps
So go Alice go, boom, boom, boom! [A7] [D]

Alice the camel has four humps ...
Alice the camel has three humps ...
Alice the camel has two humps ...
Alice the camel has one hump ...

Alice the camel has no humps
Alice the camel has no humps
Alice the camel has no humps
Because Alice is a horse of course! [A7] [D] [A7] [D]

Stand in a close circle, show five fingers.

Bend knees when singing the number of humps.

Bump neighbours hips.

Stand in a close circle, show four fingers...

Stand in a close circle, show three fingers...

Stand in a close circle, show two fingers...

Stand in a close circle, show one finger...

Hold out fist and shake head.

Show riding actions.

go
Alice
go!

17. Flipperty Flop

Flipperty Flop I'm a bullfrog ^{D} ^{A7}
Flipperty Flop I'm a bullfrog ^{D}
Flipperty Flop I'm a bullfrog ^{G}
And I'm sitting on a lily leaf pad. ^{D} ^{A7} ^{D}

Repeat

Ye har!

Jump up and down like a frog.

Crouch down.

flipperty flop!

18. BINGO

There was a farmer had a dog
[F] **[Bb]** **[F]**
And Bingo was his name O!
[C] **[F]**
B-I-N-G-O, B-I-N-G-O, B-I-N-G-O,
[F] **[Bb]** **[C]** **[F]** **[Dm]** **[Gm7]**
And Bingo was his name O!
[C7] **[F]**

Repeat.

Children join hands and dance around in a circle. Chosen child stands in the centre. At the spelling out of B-I-N-G-O children stand still. The child in the centre points to a child who should shout out the first B-I-N-G-O, and to another child for the second B-I-N-G-O. The last child who shouts out B-I-N-G-O is the next one in the centre.

39

19. Loo La Loo La

Loo la loo la loo la loo la lay
La loo la loo la loo la loo la loo la lay
Loo la loo la loo la loo la lay
La loo la loo la loo la lay.

Boo ba boo ba boo ba boo ba bay
Ba boo ba boo ba boo ba boo ba boo ba bay
Boo ba boo ba boo ba boo ba bay
Ba boo ba boo ba boo ba bay.

Too ta too ta too ta too ta tay
Ta too ta too ta too ta too ta too ta tay
Too ta too ta too ta too ta tay
Ta too ta too ta too ta tay.

Sit down in a circle.

Link arms and sway in time to the music.

Get children to suggest other actions (e.g. tap knees then clap; tap shoulders then head etc.)

20. I Feel Good

Who is loveable? [D]
I am loveable! [G]
Yes you are [A7]
And we think you're loveable too! [D]

Who is worthwhile? ...
Who is happy? ...
Who is fun? ...
Who is honest? ...
Who is kind? ...
Who is healthy? ...
Who is friendly? ...
Who is special? ...
Who is huggable? ...

Stand or sit in a circle. Open arms.

Pat your chest.

Open arms.

Join hands. Sway side to side.

Give everybody a hug!

Who is loveable ? I am loveable !

43

A message from the author...

The power of music

"Music is the la la la that lives in my mouth" (anonymous)

Music truly is one of childhood's most rewarding experiences. Here's why:-

Music is FUN!

Music/singing builds language skills

Music builds self esteem

Music helps to develop motor skills

Music builds listening, playing, creating, moving, singing and later on reading skills.

Music skills require discipline and concentration

Music can help develop warm and loving relationships (songs can be soothing, humorous, interactive)

Music helps build social skills

Musical concepts such as volume; tempo; beat and rhythm; pitch and melody; harmony and mood; and tone can be learnt.

Music is emotionally fulfilling

Linda's motto:

"You do not need to be a musical expert to share singing and dancing with children. ENTHUSIASM is the key - hang loose and enjoy the experience - children will respond whole-heartedly!"

Linda Adamson.